JOY TO THE WORLD

The Forgotten Meaning of Christmas

2013 First Printing

Joy to the World: The Forgotten Meaning of Christmas
Copyright © 2013 by Paraclete Press, Inc.

ISBN: 978-1-61261-411-3

Library of Congress Cataloging-in-Publication Data

Watts, Isaac, 1674-1748.
  Joy to the world : the forgotten meaning of Christmas / by Isaac Watts and Paraclete Press.
     pages cm
  Includes bibliographical references and index.
  ISBN 978-1-61261-411-3 (hard cover-jacket : alk. paper)
  1. Christmas poetry, English. 2. Hymns, English. I. Title.
  PR3763.W2A72 2013
  821'.5—dc23   201302108

10 9 8 7 6 5 4 3 2 1

Published by Paraclete Press
Brewster, Massachusetts
www.paracletepress.com

Printed in the United States of America

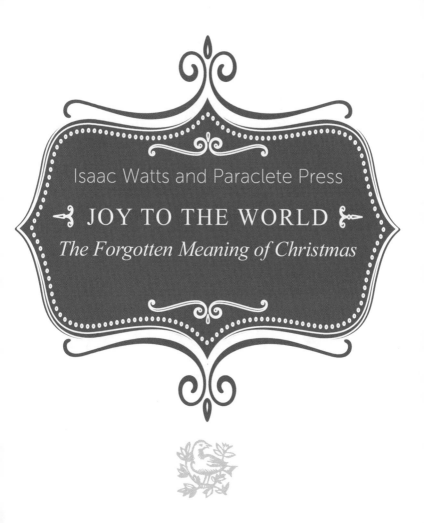

Isaac Watts and Paraclete Press

JOY TO THE WORLD

The Forgotten Meaning of Christmas

PARACLETE PRESS
BREWSTER, MASSACHUSETTS

Joy to the world! The Lord is come;

Let earth receive her King;

Let every heart prepare him room,

And heaven and nature sing,

And heaven and nature sing,

And heaven, and heaven, and nature sing.

Joy to the world! The Savior reigns;

Let men their songs employ;

While fields and floods, rocks, hills, and plains

Repeat the sounding joy,

Repeat the sounding joy,

Repeat, repeat the sounding joy.

No more let sins and sorrows grow,

Nor thorns infest the ground;

He comes to make his blessings flow

Far as the curse is found,

Far as the curse is found,

Far as, far as, the curse is found.

He rules the world with truth and grace,

And makes the nations prove

The glories of his righteousness,

And wonders of his love,

And wonders of his love,

And wonders, wonders, of his love.

JOY TO THE WORLD

⊰ CONTENTS ⊱

The Forgotten Meaning of Christmas

 he lyrics to "Joy to the World" were written in 1719 by the English Nonconformist hymn writer Isaac Watts (1674–1748).

A poet since childhood, Watts grew up to become a pastor and hymn writer. He wrote some 750 hymns and was often called, even during his own lifetime, the Father of English Hymnody.

Many of Watts's hymns are among the most familiar in the world. "From All That Dwell Below the Skies," "O God, Our Help in Ages Past," "When I Survey the Wondrous Cross," and "Alas, and Did My Savior Bleed," for instance, are found in hundreds of hymnbooks, across many Christian denominations, and sung regularly by millions in praise of God.

Watts's work was celebrated during his lifetime in England, as well as in America. Benjamin Franklin was among his earliest admirers; in fact, he was the first publisher of Watts's songs in the young American colonies in 1729.

"Joy to the World" was later put to music in 1839 by an American musician named Lowell Mason. Today, it is the most popular Christmas hymn in the world. But there's more to the story of this great hymn.

It is such a beautiful song.

Let earth receive her King!

Repeat the sounding joy!

No more let sins and sorrows grow!

He rules the world with truth and grace . . .

. . . And wonders, wonders, of his love!

Very few people know that Isaac Watts did not write "Joy to the World" to be a Christmas hymn. It was written simply to imitate one of the psalms of David: Psalm 98. Watts was working on a larger project to "retranslate" the Psalter into modern use, and he intended "Joy to the World" to inspire people to sing the words of the ancient Psalm in everyday English.

The text of the hymn was first published in 1719 in England in a volume titled *The Psalms of David Imitated in the Language of the New Testament, and Applied to the Christian State and Worship*. A writer of multiple thick volumes of sermons, theological and philosophical treatises, addresses, songs, and other translations, Isaac Watts viewed *The Psalms of David* as the major work of his life: reinterpreting the emotion, passion, and ideas of the Hebrew psalmists, infusing them with Christian theology.

He was sometimes criticized for presuming to "rewrite" a part of the Bible. How can one improve upon the already powerful language of emotion and spiritual yearning present in the Psalms? But Reverend Watts said that it was precisely because of the power in those ancient words that they ought to be rendered anew for each age—in language that will encourage people to praise God.

Praise abounds in "Joy to the World." How blessed our lives might be if we praised God with words—and songs—like this every moment of every day.

HEAVEN AND NATURE SING

REPEAT THE SOUNDING JOY

HIS BLESSINGS FLOW

GLORIES OF HIS RIGHTEOUSNESS

Watts believed that the Psalter ought to be translated differently for singing than for reading. He explained:

> The design of these two duties is very different: By reading we learn what God speaks to us in his word; but when we sing, especially unto God, our chief design is, or should be, to speak our own hearts and our words to God. . . . We breathe out our souls towards him, and make our addresses of praise and acknowledgment to him.

Perhaps this means, don't just read (or study) this book; use it to *sing*.

Watts went on, most passionately:

> It is not always necessary that our songs should be direct addresses to God; some of them may be mere meditations of the

history of divine providences, or the experiences of former saints; but even then if those providences or experiences cannot be assumed by us as parallel to our own, nor spoken in our own names, yet still there ought to be some turns of expression that may make it look at least like our own present meditation, and that may represent it as a history which we ourselves are at that time recollecting. [1]

In other words, make the words of the hymn your own.

Now, pause for a moment and read the words of David's Psalm 98 in the King James Version of the Bible that Isaac Watts knew and loved:

O sing unto the LORD a new song; for he hath done marvellous things: his right hand, and his holy arm, hath gotten him the victory.

The Lord hath made known his salvation: his
righteousness hath he openly shewed in the
sight of the heathen.

He hath remembered his mercy and his truth
toward the house of Israel: all the ends of
the earth have seen the salvation of our
God.

Make a joyful noise unto the Lord, all the
earth: make a loud noise, and rejoice, and
sing praise.

Sing unto the Lord with the harp; with the
harp, and the voice of a psalm.

With trumpets and sound of cornet make a
joyful noise before the Lord, the King.

Let the sea roar, and the fulness thereof; the
world, and they that dwell therein.

Let the floods clap their hands: let the hills
be joyful together before the Lord;
for he cometh to judge the earth: with
righteousness shall he judge the world,
and the people with equity.

Those were the words of God that inspired "Joy to the World."

When we sing Watts's new version of the Psalm, Christ's presence is assumed in those phrases. The Lord King, who is making known his righteousness, is not just God the Father, but God the Son.

"Joy to the World" is about Christ the King—even though the ancient psalmist, of course, lived centuries before Christ. How do we reconcile this?

There are some who object to inserting Christian imagery (language of the New Testament) into the Hebrew Psalms (the Old Testament). But on this point, too, Watts was adamant. These were the principles he followed:

> [The Psalms] ought to be translated in such a manner as we have reason to

believe David would have composed them if he had lived in our day. . . .

Were [David] now to transcribe them, he would make them speak the present circumstances of the church, and that in the language of the New Testament.

He would see frequent occasion to insert the cross of Christ in his song, and often underline the confessions of his sins with the blood of the Lamb.

He would often describe the glories and the triumphs of our blessed Lord in long and flowing verse, even as St. Paul, when he mentions the name and honors of Christ, can hardly part his lips from them again.[2]

Watts's approach has been summarized this way:

> While he granted that David was unquestionably a chosen instrument of God, Watts claimed that his religious understanding could not have fully apprehended the truths later revealed through Jesus Christ. The Psalms should therefore be "renovated" as if David had been a Christian.[3]

But now, look again.

You'll notice that "Joy to the World," like the original Psalm 98, actually says nothing about the coming of the Messiah as a baby. It speaks not of the Christ child—not specifically. But we know that Christ is there, don't we?

According to the vision of "Joy to the World," we sing about our God and King, the Messiah, who is victorious over evil, and comes in glory and righteousness to judge the world and comfort the faithful. This is not yet fully done. We await his coming in glory.

We know the King already; but we will soon know him completely. That is the true subject of this beloved Christmas hymn.

"Joy to the World" is meant to illuminate not so much the Advent of the Christ child, but Christ's soon-to-be, expected, triumphant return to earth.

WHAT CHRIST IS DOING AT CHRISTMAS

What a different twist this brings to our singing of a beautiful Christmas hymn. We have all the more reason to sing with joy. And as we sing—giving the anticipations of our heart's expression—we look for the consummation of what Christ is doing in, among, and all around us.

What an interesting way we might approach Advent and Christmas this year—not just celebrating the coming of the Lord as a child in Mary's arms, but as the King who has come, and will come again, in righteousness and victory.

Was there anyone there, in the Bethlehem stable, who realized what Mary and Joseph already knew? They knew, as we do when we sing "Joy to the World," that Jesus was and is the King who has come to save the world from its sins.

His coming causes us to sing with joy, but what else does it cause to happen in us? If Christ is King, what does Christmas morning mean for the world? If Christ is King, what does that mean for us, and for how we are to live our lives?

As we sing "Joy to the World," as we probably always have sung it, we are used to celebrating with our voices the Lord who has come as an infant in the manger. That is one aspect of this great story and song. But it is only one. Isaac Watts also intended his hymn to be about the second coming of Christ the King.

If you know the words of "Joy to the World," you will recognize several places in the original Psalm that inspired Isaac Watts to write what he did, and how the imagery of "Joy to the World" is well-suited to the scene on that first Christmas morning.

But Watts also creates a vision of something beyond what is only hinted at in David's Psalm. It is startling, then, that we sing the opening stanza of "Joy to the World," saying, "Let earth receive her King"—since that King of heaven and earth begins as but a baby in a stable trough. To explore this further, you will find in Chapter 5 of this book twelve days of reflections from the sermons of Isaac Watts—one set for each of the "Twelve Days of Christmas"—on what it will be like someday to see the King of Kings face-to-face.

Together, as we explore what it means to honor the King who has come, remembering and preparing for that King to come again, may we celebrate the *forgotten meaning of Christmas*.

1

Let Earth Receive Her King

Joy to the world! The Lord is come;

Let earth receive her King;

Let every heart prepare him room,

And heaven and nature sing,

And heaven and nature sing,

And heaven, and heaven, and nature sing.

hen we sing this first verse (and the second verse, as we will see) on Christmas morning, the imagery fits the occasion perfectly.

"Joy to the world! The Lord is come"—in the humblest of circumstances, when there was no room in the inn, and Joseph had to seek desperately until he was able to find only a corner of a stable in which his wife, Mary, might give birth to the Christ child.

"Let every heart prepare him room." Just as Mary and Joseph struggled to find a room in Bethlehem, it can be difficult for each of us to allow Jesus fully into our hearts. We sing with both situations in mind—one from 2,000 years ago, the other right now—in our thoughts and prayers.

"And heaven and nature sing." The angels are singing, together with the creatures in the stable and everything else that breathes, on that first Christmas morn.

Is it any wonder that we repeat, "And heaven, and heaven, and nature sing!"?

2

Let Men Their Songs Employ

Joy to the world! The Savior reigns;

Let men their songs employ;

While fields and floods, rocks, hills, and plains

Repeat the sounding joy,

Repeat the sounding joy,

Repeat, repeat the sounding joy.

 E ARE STILL IN THE HEART OF Christmas morning as we sing stanza number two.

Who doesn't think of the shepherds, for instance, when they sing, "Let men their songs employ"? Those simple men were surely wondering, mouths agape, at the events of that morning.

And we think of the landscape surrounding Bethlehem, while we intone the melodic line, "While fields and floods, rocks, hills, and plains." It all lifts up its praise to God.

Together with the attending angels, the animals, and surely Mary and Joseph, too, in the dim and quiet light of the stable, we continue to quietly "sing to the LORD a new song" (Ps. 98:1) and "Repeat the sounding joy, / Repeat the sounding joy, / Repeat, repeat the sounding joy."

3

No More Let Sins and Sorrows Grow

No more let sins and sorrows grow,

Nor thorns infest the ground;

He comes to make his blessings flow

Far as the curse is found,

Far as the curse is found,

Far as, far as, the curse is found.

WITH THIS VERSE, WE ARE TAKEN back in time to the Garden of Eden to remember the events of Genesis chapter three. It was there and then that the "sins and sorrows" first began.

The crafty serpent tempted Eve to eat the fruit of the tree in the middle of the Garden—the fruit that God had expressly forbidden. But she eats it, and she offers it to Adam, who eats of it too. Thus, sin enters the world.

"The curse" in this verse of "Joy to the World" refers to Genesis 3:14-19. "Cursed are you among all animals," God says to the serpent, and then God goes on to tell Adam and Eve the curse that sin has introduced to the world. There will be pain in childbirth, for instance, and the world will no longer be filled with bountiful trees bearing easy fruit to eat; instead, human beings will have to toil with the earth for their food, as "thorns infest the ground," in Watts's words (see Gen. 3:18).

But we sing about the coming of Christ. And that coming foretells the consummation of all things to come. Why? Because "He comes to make His blessings flow / Far as the curse is found."

4

He Rules the World with Truth and Grace

He rules the world with truth and grace,

And makes the nations prove

The glories of his righteousness,

And wonders of his love,

And wonders of his love,

And wonders, wonders, of his love.

 HEN SUDDENLY, BY THE FOURTH and final verse, we are transported to that blessed time to come when all will be fulfilled! Jesus did not remain in that manger.

He died on the cross—and then he didn't remain on the cross, either.

He rose again, sits at the right hand of God the Father, and will soon come again to judge the living and the dead. That is why we confidently sing: "He rules the world with truth and grace, / And makes the nations prove / The glories of his righteousness."

As St. Paul echoes in Philippians 2:6–11:

Who, though he was in the form of God, did not regard equality with God as something to be exploited, but emptied himself, taking the form of a slave, being born in human likeness. And being found in human form, he humbled himself and became obedient to the point of death—even death on a cross. Therefore God also highly exalted him and gave him the name that is above every name, so that at the name of Jesus every knee should bend, in heaven and on earth and under the earth, and every tongue should confess that Jesus Christ is Lord, to the glory of God the Father.

What wonders of his love indeed!

5

For the Twelve Days of Christmas

REFLECTIONS ON CHRIST THE KING
FROM THE WRITINGS
of ISAAC WATTS

Christmas Day

"Then the angel whom I saw standing on the sea and the land raised his right hand to heaven and swore by him who lives forever and ever, who created heaven and what is in it, the earth and what is in it, and the sea and what is in it: 'There will be no more delay . . .'"

— REVELATION 10:5–6

HIS IS THE OATH, AND THE solemn sentence of a mighty angel who came down from heaven and pronounced that time shall be no longer. For all seasons and times are now put into Christ's hand, together with the book of his Father's decrees. What special age or period of time in this world the prophecy refers to may not be so easy to determine, but this is certain, that it may be happily applied to the period of every person's life. For whenever the term of our continuance in this world is finished, our time, in the present circumstances and scenes that attend it, shall be no more. We shall be swept off the stage of this visible state into an unseen and eternal world. Eternity comes upon us at once, and all that we enjoy, all that we do, and all that we suffer in time, shall be no longer.

Let us stand still here, and consider, in the first place, what awful and important thoughts are contained in this sentence, what solemn ideas should arise to the view of mortal creatures, when it shall be pronounced concerning each of them that time shall be no more.

—Isaac Watts

Discourse 1—The End of Time
Discourses on the World to Come, Vol. V, 430

And I saw another mighty angel coming down from heaven, wrapped in a cloud, with a rainbow over his head; his face was like the sun, and his legs like pillars of fire. He held a little scroll open in his hand. Setting his right foot on the sea and his left foot on the land, he gave a great shout, like a lion roaring. And when he shouted, the seven thunders sounded. . . . I heard a voice from heaven saying. . . . "There will be no more delay, but in the days when the seventh angel is to blow his trumpet, the mystery of God will be fulfilled, as he announced to his servants the prophets."

—REVELATION 10:1–4, 6–7

THE SECOND DAY OF CHRISTMAS

DECEMBER 26

St. Stephen's Day

F WHAT IMPORTANCE IS IT THEN, to be frequently awakening ourselves at special seasons and periods of life, to enquire whether the image of God is begun to be renewed [in us], whether we have the glorious change wrought in us, whether our desires and delights are fixed upon holy and heavenly things, instead of those sensual and earthly objects which draw away all our souls from God and heaven.

Let it appear to us as a matter of utmost moment to seek after this change. Let us pursue it with unwearied labors and strivings with our own hearts, and perpetual importunities at the throne of grace, lest the voice of him who swears that there shall be time no longer should seize us in some unexpected moment.

—Isaac Watts

Discourse 1—The End of Time
Discourses on the World to Come, Vol. V, 431

From now on, therefore, we regard no one from a human point of view; even though we once knew Christ from a human point of view, we know him no longer in that way. So if anyone is in Christ, there is a new creation: everything old has passed away; see, everything has become new! All this is from God, who reconciled us to himself through Christ, and has given us the ministry of reconciliation; that is, in Christ God was reconciling the world to himself, not counting their trespasses against them, and entrusting the message of reconciliation to us.

—2 Corinthians 5:16–19

Feast of St. John
the Evangelist

HEN WILL THE FAITH AND COURAGE
and patience of the saints have
a blessed review. And it shall
be told before the whole creation what
strife and wrestlings a poor believer has

passed through in a dark cottage, a chamber of long sickness, or perhaps in a dungeon. How he has combatted there with powers of darkness, or struggled with huge sorrows, and has borne and not fainted, despite many temptations. Then will appear the bright scene that St. Peter represents as the event of sore trials, when our faith has been tried and is found more precious than gold. Then it will shine to the praise, honor, and glory of the suffering saints, and of Christ himself at his appearance.

—Isaac Watts

Discourse 4—Christ admired and glorified in his saints
Discourses on the World to Come, Vol. V, 526

In this you rejoice, even if now for a little while you have had to suffer various trials, so that the genuineness of your faith—being more precious than gold that, though perishable, is tested by fire—may be found to result in praise and glory and honor when Jesus Christ is revealed. Although you have not seen him, you love him; and even though you do not see him now, you believe in him and rejoice with an indescribable and glorious joy.

—1 PETER 1:6–8

Feast of the Holy Innocents

IS CHRIST EXALTED TO THE KINGDOM? Then the plots of all his enemies in earth and hell against his church are meaningless. His enemies must submit to him or perish before him. When God has set his Son Jesus as king on his holy hill of Zion (Ps. 2:1–12), it is meaningless and fruitless for anyone to speak against his kingdom.

The kings of the earth should be wise and serve the Lord in fear, bowing before him, or he will crush them with a rod of iron and throw them like a potter's vessel. The church of Christ can rejoice in her lowly estate, having such a Rule and such a Savior on high. He will never forget or forsake her interests until he has fulfilled all of his Father's promises and made her all glorious and blessed forever.

—ISAAC WATTS

SERMON XLVIII, Vol. I, 571

EXPLORE THE HOLY SCRIPTURES

Why do the nations conspire,
    and the peoples plot in vain?
The kings of the earth set themselves,
    and the rulers take counsel together,
    against the LORD and his anointed, saying,
"Let us burst their bonds asunder,
    and cast their cords from us."
He who sits in the heavens laughs;

the LORD has them in derision.
Then he will speak to them in his wrath,
  and terrify them in his fury, saying,
"I have set my king on Zion, my holy hill."
I will tell of the decree of the LORD:
He said to me, "You are my son;
  today I have begotten you.
Ask of me, and I will make the nations your
heritage,
  and the ends of the earth your possession.
You shall break them with a rod of iron,
  and dash them in pieces like a potter's vessel."
Now therefore, O kings, be wise;
  be warned, O rulers of the earth.
Serve the LORD with fear,
  with trembling kiss his feet,
or he will be angry, and you will perish in the
way;
  for his wrath is quickly kindled.
Happy are all who take refuge in him.

—PSALM 2:1–12

Feast of St. Thomas Becket

HERE IS A DAY COMING WHEN CHRIST shall make a glorious figure in the sight of men and angels. How little the saints may be esteemed in our day, looking poor and despicable in an ungodly world, yet there is an hour approaching when they will be glorious beyond all imagination, and Christ himself will be glorified in them. In that day the Lord our Savior will be the object of adoration and wonder, not only among those that have believed on him, but before all the creation.

Then it will be a fruitful spring of wonder and glory, that people of various nations and ages, of different tempers, capacities and interests, of contrary educations and contrary prejudices, will believe one gospel and trust in one deliverer from hell and death. The spritely, the studious, and the stupid, the wise and the foolish, will relish and rejoice in the same sublime truths, not only concerning the true God, but also concerning Jesus the redeemer.

— Isaac Watts

Discourse 4 — Christ admired and glorified in his saints

Discourses on the World to Come, Vol. V, 521, 522

Explore the Holy Scriptures

They sing a new song:

"You are worthy to take the scroll and to open its seals, for you were slaughtered and by your blood you ransomed for God saints from every tribe and language and people and nation; you have made them to be a kingdom and priests serving our God, and they will reign on earth."

Then I looked, and I heard the voice of many angels surrounding the throne and the living creatures and the elders; they numbered myriads of myriads and thousands of thousands, singing with full voice, "Worthy is the Lamb that was slaughtered to receive power and wealth and wisdom and might and honor and glory and blessing!" Then I heard every creature in heaven and on earth and under the earth and in the sea, and all that is in them, singing, "To the one seated on the throne and to the Lamb be blessing and honor and glory and might for ever and ever!"

—REVELATION 5:9–13

Feast of the Holy Family

STONISHING SPECTACLE! HERE will stand a believing atheist, and there a converted idolater, as monuments of the almighty power of his grace. There will shine, also, in that assembly, princes and philosophers. The princes, who love all control, will bow their scepters and their souls to the royalty and Godhead of the poor man of Nazareth. And the philosophers, who had been used to only yield to reason, will submit their understandings to divine revelation, as something above the powers and discoveries of reason.

—ISAAC WATTS

DISCOURSE 4—CHRIST ADMIRED AND GLORIFIED IN HIS SAINTS
Discourses on the World to Come, Vol. V, 522

And when he comes, he will prove the world wrong about sin and righteousness and judgment: about sin, because they do not believe in me; about righteousness, because I am going to the Father and you will see me no longer; about judgment, because the ruler of this world has been condemned. I still have many things to say to you, but you cannot bear them now. When the Spirit of truth comes, he will guide you into all the truth; for he will not speak on his own, but will speak whatever he hears, and he will declare to you the things that are to come. He will glorify me, because he will take what is mine and declare it to you. All that the Father has is mine. For this reason I said that he will take what is mine and declare it to you.

—JOHN 16:8–15

THE SEVENTH DAY OF CHRISTMAS
DECEMBER 31
Feast of St. Sylvester

OES A NEW YEAR COMMENCE, and the first morning of it dawn upon me? Let me remember that the last year was finished, and gone over my head, in order to make way for the entrance of the present. I have one year the less to travel through this world, and to fulfill the various services of a travelling state. May my diligence in duty be doubled, since the number of my appointed years is diminished.

Fix the eye of your faith on a glorified Jesus, and behold there a pattern of your own joys and glories. . . . He offered up himself a sacrifice for our sins, and thereby, according to the ancient covenant with his Father, he procured a seat of glory and power at this right hand, and eternal salvation for all his people.

—ISAAC WATTS

DISCOURSE 1—THE END OF TIME
Discourses on the World to Come, Vol. V, 487;
and Sermon XLVIII, Vol. I, 571

For you know very well that the day of the Lord will come like a thief in the night. While people are saying, "Peace and safety," destruction will come on them suddenly, as labor pains on a pregnant woman, and they will not escape. But you, brothers and sisters, are not in darkness so that this day should surprise you like a thief. You are all children of the light and children of the day. We do not belong to the night or to the darkness. So then, let us not be like others, who are asleep, but let us be awake and sober.

—1 THESSALONIANS 5:2–6 (NIV)

The Solemnity of Mary

HEN THE GREAT APPOINTED HOUR is come, and Jesus shall return from heaven with a shout of the archangel and the trumpet of God (1 Thess. 4:16), then he will call up his saints from their bed of dust and darkness and make the graves resign those prisoners of hope. Then they will all gather together around their Lord, a bright and numerous army, shining and reflecting the splendors of his presence. How will the judgment of flesh and sense be confounded at once, and reversed with shame! "Is this the man that was loaded with scandal, that was buffeted with scorn, and scourged, and crucified in the land of Judea? Is this the person that hung on the cursed tree and expired under agonies of pain and sorrow? How majestic, how divine his appearance! The Son of God and the king of glory!"

—ISAAC WATTS

DISCOURSE 4—CHRIST ADMIRED
AND GLORIFIED IN HIS SAINTS
Discourses on the World to Come, Vol. V, 531-32

According to the Lord's word, we tell you that we who are still alive, who are left until the coming of the Lord, will certainly not precede those who have fallen asleep. For the Lord himself will come down from heaven, with a loud command, with the voice of the archangel and with the trumpet call of God, and the dead in Christ will rise first. After that, we who are still alive and are left will be caught up together with them in the clouds to meet the Lord in the air. And so we will be with the Lord forever. Therefore encourage one another with these words.

—1 Thessalonians 4:15–18 (niv)

THE NINTH DAY OF CHRISTMAS
JANUARY 2

E IS COME, HE IS COME," SAYS the saint, that same Lord Jesus whom I have seen, whom I have known, and loved in the days of my mortal life, whom I have long waited for in the dust of death. He is come to reward all my labors, to wipe away all my sorrows, to finish my faith and turn it into sight, to fulfill all my hopes and his own promises. He is come to deliver me forever from all my enemies, and to bear me to the place which he has prepared for those that love him and long for his appearance.

O blessed be the God of grace, who has convinced me of the sins of my nature, and the sins of my life in the days of my flesh; who has discovered to me the danger of a guilty and sinful state, has shown me the commission of mercy in the hands of his Son, has pointed me to the Lamb of God who was offered as a sacrifice to take away our sins, and has inclined me to receive him in all his divine characters and offices, and to follow the captain of my salvation through all the labors and dangers of life. I have trusted in him, I have loved him, I have endeavored through many frailties to honor and obey him, and I can now behold his face.

—ISAAC WATTS
DISCOURSE 6—THE VAIN REFUGE
OF SINNERS
Discourses on the World to Come, Vol. V, 554

————⊶⊷⊶⊶⊷⊶⊷⊶————

But their minds were hardened. Indeed, to this very day, when they hear the reading of the old covenant, that same veil is still there, since only in Christ is it set aside. Indeed, to this very day whenever Moses is read, a veil lies over their minds; but when one turns to the Lord, the veil is removed. Now the Lord is the Spirit, and where the Spirit of the Lord is, there is freedom. And all of us, with unveiled faces, seeing the glory of the Lord as though reflected in a mirror, are being transformed into the same image from one degree of glory to another; for this comes from the Lord, the Spirit.

—2 Corinthians 3:14–18

Feast of St. Genevieve

HILE THE MIGHTY PEOPLE OF THE earth tremble with amazement, and call to the rocks and mountains to hide them from his face, I rejoice to see him in his robes of judgment, for he is come to pronounce me righteous in the face of men and angels, to declare me a good and faithful servant before the whole creation, to set the crown of victory on my head, to take me to heaven with him, that where he is I may be also, to behold his glory, and to partake forever of the blessings of his love. Amen.

When the soul is arrived at heaven, we shall be all warm and fervent in our divine and delightful work. As there will be nothing painful to the senses in that blessed climate, so there will not be one cold heart there, nor so much as one luke-warm worshipper. For we will live under the immediate rays of God, who formed the light, and under the kindest influences of Jesus, the sun of righteousness. We will be made like his angels, who are most active spirits, and his ministers, who are flames of fire.

—ISAAC WATTS

DISCOURSE 6—THE VAIN REFUGE
OF SINNERS
Discourses on the World to Come, Vol. V, 554;
and
DISCOURSE 7—NO NIGHT IN HEAVEN
Discourses on the World to Come, Vol. V, 559

Jesus . . . looked up to heaven and said, . . . "The glory that you have given me I have given them, so that they may be one, as we are one, I in them and you in me, that they may become completely one, so that the world may know that you have sent me and have loved them even as you have loved me. Father, I desire that those also, whom you have given me, may be with me where I am, to see my glory, which you have given me because you loved me before the foundation of the world.

"Righteous Father, the world does not know you, but I know you; and these know that you have sent me. I made your name known to them, and I will make it known, so that the love with which you have loved me may be in them, and I in them."

—JOHN 17:1, 22–26

Feast of St. Elizabeth Ann Seton

 HE INHERITANCE OF THE SAINTS, in light, is sufficiently irradiated by God himself, who at his first call made the light spring up out of darkness over a wide chaos of confusion, before the sun and moon appeared, and the beams of divine light, grace and glory, are communicated from God, the original fountain of it, by the Lamb to all the inhabitants of the heavenly country. It was by Jesus, his Son, that God made the light at first, and by him he conveys it to all the happy worlds.

The spirits of the just are made perfect. This is one of their privileges, that they go to dwell, not only where they see the face of God, but where they behold the glory of Christ, and converse with Jesus, the mediator of the new covenant (Heb. 12:23–24), and are forever with the Lord who redeemed them (2 Cor. 5:8).

—ISAAC WATTS

DISCOURSE 7—NO NIGHT IN HEAVEN
Discourses on the World to Come, Vol. V, 560

But you have come to Mount Zion and to the city of the living God, the heavenly Jerusalem, and to innumerable angels in festal gathering, and to the assembly of the firstborn who are enrolled in heaven, and to God the judge of all, and to the spirits of the righteous made perfect, and to Jesus, the mediator of a new covenant, and to the sprinkled blood that speaks a better word than the blood of Abel.

See that you do not refuse the one who is speaking; for if they did not escape when they refused the one who warned them on earth, how much less will we escape if we reject the one who warns from heaven!

—Hebrews 12:22–25

The Day Before Epiphany

LESSED BE GOD THAT THE NIGHT of ignorance, grief, or affliction that attends us in this world is not everlasting night. Heaven and glory are at hand. Wait and watch for the morning star, for Jesus, and the resurrection.

Roll on apace in your appointed course, you suns and moons, and all you twinkling enlighteners of the sky, carry on the changing seasons of light and darkness in this lower world with your utmost speed until you have finished all my appointed months of continuance here.

The light of faith shows me the dawning of that glorious day that shall finish all my nights and darknesses forever.

Make haste, O delightful morning, and delay not my hopes.

Let me hasten, let me arrive at that blessed inheritance, those mansions of paradise, where night is never known, but one eternal day shall make our knowledge, our holiness, and our joy eternal. Amen.

—ISAAC WATTS

DISCOURSE 7—NO NIGHT IN HEAVEN
Discourses on the World to Come, Vol. V, 564-5

EXPLORE THE HOLY SCRIPTURES

Blessed be the God and Father of our Lord Jesus Christ! By his great mercy he has given us a new birth into a living hope through the resurrection of Jesus Christ from the dead, and into an inheritance that is imperishable, undefiled, and unfading, kept in heaven for you, who are being protected by the power of God through faith for a salvation ready to be revealed in the last time. In this you rejoice, even if now for a little while you have had to suffer various trials, so that the genuineness of your faith—being more precious than gold that, though perishable, is tested by fire—may be found to result in praise and glory and honor when Jesus Christ is revealed. Although you have not seen him, you love him; and even though you do not see him now, you believe in him and rejoice with an indescribable and glorious joy, for you are receiving the outcome of your faith, the salvation of your souls.

—1 Peter 1:3–9

Appendix

More Christmas Hymns about the Second Coming

SAAC WATTS WASN'T THE FIRST to begin what was once a rich tradition of writing songs to imitate the Hebrew Psalms. The Swiss reformer John Calvin was the first, in Geneva in the early sixteenth century; he wanted to encourage his otherwise stoic congregations to actually sing during worship!

There may have been as many as seventy complete and partial versions of the Psalter published in vernacular verse, suitable for singing, before Isaac Watts ever wrote and published his own in 1719. [4]

Sprinkled throughout these various versions are Advent and Christmas hymns that are simultaneously looking to the Incarnation of Christ and awaiting his second coming.

Reproduced below are a few popular examples over the centuries.

Charles Wesley, for instance, wrote the following song after the same Psalm 98 that inspired Isaac Watts to write "Joy to the World." It is similar to "Joy to the World," with imagery that refers to both the first and second comings of Christ. We have not sung this one in church for centuries probably simply because no one ever put the words to a melodious tune!

Sing We to Our Conquering Lord

[VERSES 1, 2, 6, AND 7]

BY CHARLES WESLEY

Sing we to our conquering Lord

A new triumphant song;

Joyfully his deeds record,

And with a thankful tongue:

Wonders his right hand hath wrought;

Still his outstretch'd arm we see;

He alone the fight hath fought,

And got the victory.

God, the' almighty God, hath made

His great salvation known;

Openly to all display'd

His glory in his Son:

Christ hath brought the life to light,

Bade the glorious gospel shine,

Show'd, in all the Heathen's sight,

His righteousness Divine.

Ocean, roar, with all thy waves,
In honour of his Name;
He who all creation saves
Doth all their homage claim:
Clap your hands, ye floods! Ye hills,
Joyful all his praise rehearse;
Praise him till his glory fills
The vocal universe!

Lo! he comes with clouds! He comes
In dreadful pomp array'd!
All his glorious power assumes,
To judge the world he made:
Righteous shall his sentences be:
Think of that tremendous bar!
Every eye the Judge shall see!
And *thou* shalt meet him there!

This other popular hymn by Charles Wesley
is sung in thousands of churches every Advent
season. The song depicts the entire life of Christ,

never mentioning the coming in the stable,
focusing entirely on the Kingship of our Lord.

Lo! He Comes, with Clouds Descending

BY CHARLES WESLEY

Lo! he comes, with clouds descending,
once for our salvation slain;
thousand thousand saints attending
swell the triumph of his train:
Alleluia! alleluia! alleluia!
Christ the Lord returns to reign.

Every eye shall now behold him,
robed in dreadful majesty;
those who set at nought and sold him,
pierced, and nailed him to the tree,
deeply wailing, deeply wailing, deeply wailing,
shall the true Messiah see.

Those dear tokens of his passion
still his dazzling body bears,

cause of endless exultation

to his ransomed worshipers;

with what rapture, with what rapture,

with what rapture

gaze we on those glorious scars!

Now redemption, long expected,

see in solemn pomp appear;

all his saints, by man rejected,

now shall meet him in the air:

Alleluia! alleluia! alleluia!

See the day of God appear!

Yea, amen! let all adore thee,

high on thine eternal throne;

Savior, take the power and glory;

claim the kingdom for thine own:

Alleluia! alleluia! alleluia!

Thou shalt reign, and thou alone.

And then there is this beautiful hymn, written by Martin Luther in 1523 and later put to memorable music by Johann Sebastian Bach, praising the Child in the manger, while never forgetting the King and Kingship that are forever his.

Savior of the Nations, Come

BY MARTIN LUTHER

Savior of the nations, come;
Virgin's Son, here make Thy home!
Marvel now, O heaven and earth,
That the Lord chose such a birth.

Not by human flesh and blood;
By the Spirit of our God
Was the Word of God made flesh,
Woman's offspring, pure and fresh.

Wondrous birth! O wondrous Child
Of the virgin undefiled!
Though by all the world disowned,
Still to be in heaven enthroned.

From the Father forth He came
And returneth to the same,
Captive leading death and hell
High the song of triumph swell!

Thou, the Father's only Son,
Hast over sin the victory won.
Boundless shall Thy kingdom be;
When shall we its glories see?

Brightly doth Thy manger shine,
Glorious is its light divine.
Let not sin o'er cloud this light;
Ever be our faith thus bright.

Praise to God the Father sing,
Praise to God the Son, our King,
Praise to God the Spirit be
Ever and eternally.

Notes

1 All notes are references to the works of Isaac Watts, taken from *The Works of the Rev. Isaac Watts, D.D. in Seven Volumes* (Leeds, England: Printed by Edward Baines, no date, but ca. 1800). This quote comes from "A Short Essay toward the Improvement of Psalmody," Vol. VII, p. 5.

2 *The Works of the Rev. Isaac Watts,* "A Short Essay toward the Improvement of Psalmody," Vol. VII, p. 9.

3 Stephen A. Marini, *Sacred Song in America: Religion, Music, and Public Culture* (Urbana, IL: University of Illinois Press, 2003), 76.

4 See for instance, the annotated list in the "Supplement" to Henry Fish's (ed.) *A Poetical Version of Nearly the Whole of The Psalms of David, Second Edition*, by the Rev. Charles Wesley (London: Henry Fish, 1854), 300–20.

About Paraclete Press

Recordings   From Gregorian chant to contemporary American choral works, our music recordings celebrate sacred choral music through the centuries. Paraclete distributes the recordings of the internationally acclaimed choir Gloriæ Dei Cantores, praised for their "rapt and fathomless spiritual intensity" by *American Record Guide*, and the Gloriæ Dei Cantores Schola, which specializes in the study and performance of Gregorian chant. Paraclete is also the exclusive North American distributor of the recordings of the Monastic Choir of St. Peter's Abbey in Solesmes, France, long considered to be a leading authority on Gregorian chant.

Videos   Our videos offer spiritual help, healing, and biblical guidance for life issues: grief and loss, marriage, forgiveness, anger management, facing death, and spiritual formation.

Learn more about us at our website:

www.paracletepress.com,

or call us toll-free at 1-800-451-5006.

SCAN
TO
READ
MORE

O Christmas Three

BY O. HENRY, TOLSTOY, AND DICKENS

$16.99 | Hardcover | ISBN 978-1-55725-776-5

This beautiful gift book contains three heart-warming stories that recall Christmases past:

- O. Henry's all-American tale, "The Gift of the Magi," originally published in 1906.
- Leo Tolstoy's Russian folktale, "Where Love Is, There God Is Also" from 1887.
- Charles Dickens' little known classic, "What Christmas Is, As We Grow Older," 1851.

The Story of the Other Wise Man

BY HENRY VAN DYKE

$14.95 | Hardcover | ISBN: 978-1-55725-610-2

One of the most meaningful stories ever written...

Henry van Dyke's Christmas classic is told in the manner of the great fairy tales—and like a great fairy tale, it couldn't be more true! This beautiful edition is designed so that you can read *The Other Wise Man* as it is intended to be read—slowly.

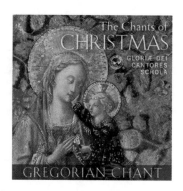

The Chants of Christmas

GLORIÆ DEI CANTORES SCHOLA

$16.95 CD | ISBN: 978-1-61261-377-2

This Christmas, give the gift of music—the earliest, purest music of the Church. Gregorian chant lifts us out of the ordinary stresses of life and invites us to contemplate the timeless and unchanging love of God. Includes Christmas Day Mass.

Available from most booksellers
or through Paraclete Press:

www.paracletepress.com   1-800-451-5006

Try your local bookstore first.